MW00526536

More Than a
Coincidence:

True Stories *of*
Divine Intervention

Compiled *by*
JOYCE KOCINSKI

For Mom & Dad,
my Angels in heaven

Contents

Introduction

DID YOU EVER FEEL a time in your life when things just fell into place as part of some Divine plan? How many events can happen by "chance" until we realize there is a path we must follow? When will we recognize that sometimes there are angels watching over us? I hope the stories you are about to read will inspire you to notice the miracles around you that happen every day. We all have experienced events in our lives that seem to be "more than a coincidence" and we sometimes stop and wonder if it was Divine intervention. My purpose for compiling these stories is to bring more people closer to God and realize how much He cares for us. Perhaps you may have a story to share as well. Please contact Joyce Kocinski at jkocinski@wowway.com for more information.

1

Faith That Heals

Be of good courage, and he shall strengthen your heart,
all ye that hope in the Lord.

~ Psalms 31:24

†

Signs from God

~ submitted by Gary Renard,
grandson of Ella Renard

IT WAS 1923 AND my husband, Al, and I lived on a farm near
Momence, Illinois, with our four sons, Donald, who at 11 was the
oldest, 9-year-old Dale; 7-year-old C.J and my 3-year-old baby boy,
Bob.

Donald came home from school one Friday; he was very sick.
He said his stomach hurt. He didn't eat much at supper and hardly
any breakfast the next day. He was very thirsty and because I, like
many other farm people, didn't have a thermometer, it never
occurred to me he might have a fever. He lay in bed all day
Saturday and didn't want anyone to bother him. I wanted my
husband to call the doctor but he said he thought there was
nothing wrong. I argued he was sick but my husband said if
Donald eats, he will feel better.

I thought maybe it was his appendix that was bothering him.
Al said, "Don't worry he will be all right in a few days."

Sunday, Donald lay in bed all day and drank gallons of water. I continued to worry and that night, he suddenly woke up and said, "Mama, can I spit at the tree?"

He was delirious and little did I know at that time, his appendix had burst. I got up, covered him and was alarmed at his condition. Monday, my husband still refused to accept how serious Donald's condition was; Donald had not eaten in three days.

Tuesday morning, I told my husband, "Just look at that child! He looks like a ghost." His eyes were large and sunk in, his nose pinched whiter than a dead person. "Al, should I should get him ready and we will take him into town?" Finally, Al relented.

When we got to the doctor's office, the doctor gave one look at Donald and told Al to put the boy on the table. He said he had a ruptured appendix and peritonitis. He told us to rush him to the hospital to be operated on immediately.

The hospital was St. Mary's in Kankakee, so we had to leave Dale and C.J. home alone. I took Bob with me because he was only three. They operated on Donald and sent him back to his room. My husband asked the doctor, what are his chances? The doctor replied, "Where there is life, there is hope." He asked him again for the "straight truth" and the doctor looked grim and said, "Mr. Renard, I can't tell you one way or the other as it is up to God now."

The next morning when I visited Donald, he was delirious. His fever was 107 degrees, I was told. I overheard the nurses talking in the hall. I stayed day and night by his side for three days. One night one of the nurses said to me the crisis was soon to break one way or another. We waited, and I felt peaceful. I was sitting on a bench and prayed, "Heavenly Father, please don't take my son! Who I am to ask because You didn't spare Your Son for us."

Then a robin landed on the open window ledge and sang as if its little heart would burst. It seemed to be a sign from God telling me that Donald would live.

I said to the little bird, "I know you are happy, and I am happy, too, that my little boy will live." Then I burst into tears.

I quickly went to Donald's room and a nurse shushed me and said, "He is asleep, and he is going to be all right."

I gave Donald to God, and He gave him back to me.

Twice Blessed by Michael

~ Peg Ricketts

TUTORING A DARLING PRESCHOOLER with autism was becoming a real challenge for me. Although I loved working with Michael, I had been feeling ill and restless for nearly six months.

The patience and focus I needed were no longer there. I had sought answers from many doctors for my fatigue and red, angry bruises on my trunk and legs. Although they didn't say so, I believed they each thought I was a crazy, menopausal woman. I continued to pray and search for answers. A week after my monthly breast check, a lump suddenly grew in my breast. I had it removed and was assured by the surgeon it was "just a fibro adenoma." He said he had excised hundreds of them, but would send it to the lab. Hearing nothing for 3 weeks, I assumed he was right. Imagine my angst when his office called and said he wanted to see me within an hour. It was Friday, and he was leaving town. The biopsy "looked like cancer," but was not conclusive. He made an appointment with an oncologist for the following week.

At that meeting I was told it was probably Non-Hodgkin's lymphoma (NHL). Still, I had no definite diagnosis. Waiting and praying consumed my days and nights. I told Our Lord I was willing to travel this road, but needed something to hold onto; to assure me He was with me.

During this waiting time, Michael's other tutor Shannon brought him over for a visit. Michael had a very limited vocabulary but loved rolling around on what he called my "water bed." He had struggled to learn and then put those two words together.

Knowing he would spend a good half hour or more in the bed, Shannon and I visited in the living room. Michael walked out a few minutes later and handed me a Bible verse I had written out on a small Christmas notepad many years earlier. I often wrote verses on Post-it notes, but this was special paper our family Christmas Elf used to write Advent notes to our kids. They were all grown and gone, and I had not seen the paper for years. I didn't recall writing it, and have no idea where he found it, but as he handed it to me, he said, "Here, Peggy," strong and clear. My heart nearly stopped as I read:

I will set you on high because you acknowledge My Name.
You will call upon Me and I will answer you. I will be with
you in your distress. I will deliver you and glorify you.
With length of days I will gratify you and will show you
My salvation. ~ Psalm 91:14-16

That was fourteen years ago. The diagnosis was Stage IV NHL. I went through chemo and became a volunteer with the hospital and related cancer organizations. Life was good and I was sharing hope and encouragement with many patients.

Four years into this, two weeks after our son was deployed to Iraq, the tension headaches I was having turned out to be a brain tumor, a recurrence of NHL. I began treatment again. Our daughter, Mary, was pregnant with our first grandchild. I wanted to be here for that great event, and to welcome Terry home when his tour ended.

Traveling through Iraq in convoys to flush out insurgents, Terry would call home when he could. We treasured these short visits. He would always end the call saying "We are both fighting wars, Mom. You keep your head up, and I'll keep my head down."

I ended up needing a bone marrow (stem cell) transplant. After three months of chemo, they removed "clean" stem cells from my bone marrow and froze them until I was strong enough to have the transplant. Standard protocol is four days of high dose chemo to wipe out all stem cells, and then the ones they removed go back into my blood.

My sister Cookie came to the hospital each night to be there for me. She told me later I called Terry's name repeatedly during the night. I was very weak and she didn't think I'd survive all of this. She didn't want me to die alone.

The day I was released from the hospital, my husband Pat came in my room with tears rolling down his cheeks. I sunk into the bed. Terry had been shot in an ambush. He had been trapped in his burning truck. Convoys under attack are to keep moving. A female soldier broke protocol and rescued him. She is half his size. I am so thankful God used her for him. His injuries were enough to bring him home. We healed together.

Our beautiful granddaughter, Aaliyah, will be ten on Feb 21st. When she was three weeks old, she had her hands folded (as if in prayer) when my transplant took place. She has an eight-year-old sister, Monica. I will celebrate ten years cancer-free March 7th, 2015! By the way, my friend Michael's birthday is March 7th.

Terry is healthy and doing well. He is a parole officer for the state of Nebraska. He brings strength, courage and hope to his parolees.

I still do volunteer work with cancer patients. We praise God for our lives and for using us to share His love.

Never Give Up Hope

~ *Cristina Ybarra*

IT WAS JUNE 2011 and I was nearing the bottom of my drinking career.

As an ICU nurse, I learned "you work hard, you play hard." Well, that's a great justification for this alcoholic! It's that kind thinking which continued my behavior into my second DUI offense, being $30,000 in debt, on the verge of losing my job, and multiple future ramifications to come. I was in the rampant path to self destruction. I wanted to die ... and I didn't see a way out. I realized I was deep trouble. I couldn't figure out what went wrong. Was I seeking God at all? No! *I got this, God! Besides, I'm angry at you anyways and vice versa.* You know ... love hate relationship, right? Well I'm broke and alone. What to do? What to do? I know! I am going to work myself to death and drink to mask my pain. Let me get right on this masterpiece of a plan.

While I was concocting my plans to get out of debt, God had his own agenda for my life.

I was manically trying to work to make up for my large pile of debt overnight. It was an insane morning at the hospital and I was putting out fires left and right from low blood pressures to stroke victims. My last stop that morning was a patient named Dan and my first thought was *damn! Bad idea to triple this morning,* I thought to myself.

I took one look at Dan and spoke to his wife, Karen, and warned her that her husband was in trouble. He was extremely short of breath and on a noninvasive breathing machine. I told her she needed to call for prayers. The next few hours involved stabilizing Dan and putting him on life support. I ran my rear end off and didn't leave the hospital until 11 o'clock that night.

The next two weeks I developed a relationship with Karen as she faithfully came to visit her husband daily. There was just something about her spirit. She was just unshaken. I was curious about the peace she had. This was something foreign to me and my chaotic nature. As we were waiting for Dan's body to come around, I watched her faithfulness and culture of prayer. Her church family would come and pray over Dan daily. Something then just started to finally feel right.

Dan was on full life support for two weeks and now on multiple machines and drips to keep his failing organs going. I wasn't sure how much time Dan had left. The doctors wanted Karen to make decisions about making Dan comfortable and letting him pass. I was then off a few days and had time to regroup. It was a lot for me to process. I didn't want him to die! Then something came upon me to start praying for him. I even starting bargaining with God. I genuinely asked for healing on his heart as a birthday present to me. Just like that, it was the beginning of my miracle. I came back to work and witnessed over the next few weeks a man being brought back to life by the hands of his Creator. Amazing!

In between my encounter with Dan and Karen, I was forced to take time off work, go to rehab, and become the sober person I had missed for so long. I had always felt like I was somehow lying to them because they didn't know my dirty little secrets, but the Holy Spirit guided me into telling them and I just felt love and acceptance from them. No judgment ... just compassion for my situation. After all, I then came to know Dan's struggles with alcoholism and that he has been sober for twenty-plus years. Aren't we a pair made in heaven? Felt like it. They showed me God through their character and love.

Dan has now made a full recovery and has returned to back to work. He is still an active member in Alcoholics Anonymous and in pretty good health, despite his near-death experience. What that man went through, I can't even imagine. All this time, he had been out of it and I was a stranger, but to his family their angel. He was a miracle man indeed.

I still remember when he came to and realized what had happened. He tells me the most touching words I wasn't expecting: "I would do it all again because I know it meant salvation for you." Now that's some power! This man suffered greatly, but was willing to re-embark that journey to help someone know Jesus.

This story couldn't have been any more perfect. God brings people in our lives for a reason. That is how I know in my heart that this was God trying to get my attention and bring me back him to fulfill his purpose for me. For it is God's loving kindness that leads us to repentance (Romans 2:4). He loved me so much that he protected and brought me back into relationship with him.

I can say all I want that I was searching for God, but we never really do. God is always seeking us whether we like to admit it or not. I have more peace and joy in my life. I now know that He has begun a good work in me. Tune in later because God's not finished with me yet and I'm still here! Amen!

2

Heeding the Signs

In all thy ways acknowledge him,
and he shall direct thy paths.

~ Proverbs 3:6

†

Knowing When to Trust

~ Joyce Kocinski

"MAYBE ONE OF YOUR brothers will have a place for me at their house," Dad said one day when I was visiting him in Phoenix. He moved there when he retired. His memory was getting worse and he was not aware the family had already decided on a nursing home for him.

After he was diagnosed with Alzheimer's disease a year before, my brothers, sisters and I had some family meetings to discuss what to do. My preference was an in-home caregiver like the Polish one my husband had found for his father. We visited several nursing homes and my brothers liked one close by Dad's condo. There was a separate unit for Alzheimer's residents with a family-like atmosphere. Dad would be able to socialize with the other residents, and Betty was close by to visit him.

Betty was the special person in Dad's life he met when he moved to Phoenix. It was his dream to retire to a warm climate but not my mother's. She chose to stay in Chicago to be near us, her six children and ten grandchildren.

It was sad to see him move so far away but he visited us a few times a year. He seemed happy and relaxed in his new life but I could tell he still missed us. There were his weekly letters and phone calls. "Arizona calling!" was the message he left on my answering machine.

At 80, he became more forgetful, not remembering to take his medication or eating well. The diagnosis of Alzheimer's affected all of us. We knew we had to make some hard decisions. At first, I asked, "Why him?" Then I answered, "Why not him?" Who gets to choose when illness occurs? Should we move him back home? There were mixed feelings but we decided as a family it would be unfair to Betty. She was like his second wife and to separate them would be traumatic for both of them.

Betty gradually took over the daily chores for him. She cooked, cleaned, and ran errands, took him to his doctor's appointments. Since we were so many miles away, it was a blessing to know Betty was there for him. Still, it was difficult talking to him and keeping in touch.

Gradually, he stopped writing to us as his memory became worse. He would call us two or three times a day and not remember he had already talked to us. I continued to write to him since he could still read and enjoy the news I shared.

When I came to visit, he enjoyed spending time with me and we would go on daily walks. When he saw family photos in his albums, he couldn't recognize them. I labeled each picture to help him remember. I made a chart with photos of my siblings next to their phone number for his convenience. The more I read about his disease, the more understanding and patient I became.

His condition got worse, and he would get angry and combative when he felt threatened or confused. Once I got a call from a stranger in Phoenix who had stopped to help Dad. "Your father was asking me for directions to drive to Chicago," he said. Luckily, my phone number was in his wallet.

I called Betty to come get him and told my brother, "It's time to take his car away." That was a sad day for him and he had a hard time accepting it. During one of my visits, I heard him get up at 3 a.m., get dressed and readied to leave the house. "Dad," I said, "Please give me the keys. It's not time to get up! It's still dark outside." He reluctantly handed them over, confused, and I went to bed, concerned how he was losing touch. I prayed for the strength I needed to get through this time with him.

We decided not to tell Dad when he was moving until the last minute as he only forgot and it would upset him. The last week before his move to the home, we had a family dinner and took some pictures. That week while I was staying with him, I started cleaning my dad's condo in preparation for the move.

In the kitchen, I threw out old food from the pantry. There was little left in the cabinets as each time we visited Dad we bought the food we would eat for that week. The refrigerator was empty except for some water bottles. Memories of some of the happy family meals from previous visits surfaced in my mind.

I glanced at the family photos in the dining room. There was the one of us children standing around Dad in the back yard long ago. There was the Christmas photo of Dad surrounded by his grandchildren. I sat in Dad's recliner and looked out the window where he used to feed the birds. I saw the trees and some birds, but the view was different. The condo felt empty.

While working in the condo and worrying about my father in the nursing home, I got a phone call from my sister. My mother was in the hospital again. Two months previous, she had fallen and broken her leg. After surgery, and recovery time in rehabilitation, she moved in with me. One night I heard a noise at midnight and checked on her. She was pale and nauseous so I called 911. She had a heart attack! She spent the next several months in and out of hospital and now was back in again.

I started getting chest pains. The stress was too much for me.

There I was, 1,400 miles away worrying about both my parents, overwhelmed with stress. I opened the kitchen cabinet and saw a coffee mug on the shelf. Printed on it were the words, "Be still and know that I am God!" The mug was a gift I had given to my father at one point. It was a reminder at that moment to calm down and stop worrying. "Be still and know that I am God." I felt that was a sign things would work out, and I started to relax. The pains subsided. God was saying, "Trust in Me." I calmed down and realized who was really in charge.

Taking a Chance

~ Sarah Bennett

ALMOST A YEAR AGO, after my second baby was born, I made the scary decision to quit my job of more than seven years to stay home with my two young children. I did this in the worst economy of my life and second-guessed myself numerous times after doing so.

Things were not easy living in a two-income world with two children and three cats to feed, and a mortgage. It was during this time that my faith in God has deepened more than ever before. Just when we needed something, it would appear.

For example, I bought tickets for a charity raffle and won. The prizes were gymnastics classes for my daughter, tickets to a comedy club the weekend before my wedding anniversary, tickets to an amusement park just when I was feeling down, tickets for numerous restaurants to eat for free, and some amazing artwork that I never would have been able to afford. This was more than just a coincidence.

Around the same time, a neighbor down the street was giving away a brand new riding tractor for free. It just needed a little work and we were able to sell our old John Deer with 470 hours on it for a mower with 40 hours.

We also were able to refinance and lower our mortgage payment $100 to the lowest interest rate in recent history of less than 4 percent! They told us at the time that it would cost $400 for the appraisal and when we went to refinance they said that they miscalculated and gave us a check for $1,000! Just when we needed the cash!

I had bought a used car that continually broke down a few years ago and won a settlement in a class action suit. My share came to over $2,000!

Overall, too many things were happening to name it just a coincidence. Now that I sense my time home with my children may be coming to an end I look back on this year. It will always stand out to me as a sign that no matter how desperate or impossible something might seem at the time, God will bring you through it. Living the life of full-time working mother and now stay-at-home mother, I have gotten to experience both sides and come to a greater appreciation for all mothers struggling in this world to raise their children to the best of their ability.

My message is this after this experience: I do believe in God and that the lessons that we learn are not always easy but in the end for the best. One quote that stuck with me is "Do not lean unto your own understanding." Trust that "all things work for the goodness of God."

Signs

~ *Gary Renard*

I HAD PICKED THE wrong week to quarrel with Mr. B, our department director. He gave me an unpaid three-day suspension, and I countered with my two-week resignation notice. I was joining the long line of other managers who had either been fired or quit under Mr. B's heavy-handed direction.

In my final week there, a package of books came from a Christian book company in Fargo, North Dakota. It had arrived by regular mail and I noticed it was postmarked on Saturday, July 22. How strange was that—that this package could arrive at our little post office in Hampshire, Illinois, in a day and a half?

Whatever the reason, the feeling came upon me gradually and then strongly that I needed to pray, and not just in a time of quiet mediation or reflection on the Scriptures, but in a very real and powerful sense that for one hour, I was going to be in the Presence of God. I hadn't felt anything like this before. I was nervous and shaky, but as I knelt, I simply had a heart-to heart conversation with God. I told him that I was sorry I'd lost my temper and made such a mess of my previous job. Wherever He would lead me next, I would do my best to live a message of peace.

As I came into work the next morning, my supervisor took me aside and said, "Have you got a minute? There's something I need to tell you." He closed the door behind us and said, "Mr. B is gone. The president has giving him his notice, and he isn't coming back. Now I know you've given your notice and this is your last week, but if you want to change your mind, I wish you'd stay. It's up to you."

I could feel the blood draining from my face. I felt like I was going to pass out.

"My Lord and my God!" I thought. I knew this was His answer; I was struck through with fear. In that moment, God wasn't just the subject of some long ago Bible stories, but One who was powerfully present, right here, right now.

Later that day, my supervisor asked that whenever I had time, to get a couple of cartons and clean out Mr. B's desk. As I was doing this, I thought of how ironic this was, that I was getting rid of things that belonged to the man who was going to be rid of me.

Later that evening, I was still shaky as I prayed. "OK, Lord, you got my attention! Now what do you want me to do? Whatever it is, I am eternally Yours."

I had just listened to a recorded sermon in which a pastor told of the unexpected ways that God answers prayer.

"How do we know that these answers are really from God, and not just our imagination?" the pastor asked. "Because God will give you a sign of confirmation. Here is what I found; everywhere I go to speak as a pastor, I find roses. Whenever I see them, I know they are God's sign of confirmation to me. That's my sign. What's yours?"

"Hmm," I thought. "What would I ask for a sign of confirmation?" Then I thought, no, I wouldn't ask for such a sign, because that would be putting God to the test. The question kept nagging me. What if I really wanted to ask God for a sign because I was in a dire situation? In that case, I would ask for roses.

The next day I went about my job. It was a sunny but windy and very cold day in February. As I crossed the street, there in the snow lay two fresh pink miniature roses.

"Wow," I thought. "How strange is that?! What are the chances of finding fresh roses in the snow? They must have fallen from somebody's floral arrangement."

As soon as I picked them up, I recalled the message of God's sign in the sermon from the day before. I'd said I would not ask for them, but here they were, just the same.

Later I recalled the passage in Isaiah 7:

"I will not ask for a sign," said King Ahaz. "I will not put my God to the test." Even if you will not ask, God, Himself will give you a sign.

The Bible Study

~ Joyce Kocinski

I HAVE ATTENDED A weekly bible study class with other women at a Catholic church for the past two years. I enjoy getting together with them to socialize and learn about my faith. Although a "cradle" Catholic, I never felt I took enough time to read the Bible or learn from the various stories in the Old or New Testaments.

In this class, we meet as a whole group to share our prayer intentions, good news, and updates on church events. Then after that, we count off by threes or fours, and we break up into smaller groups to discuss the chapter in the book we are studying. Caring women volunteer in the church nursery to help take care of young children that some of the women bring to this class.

On this day, as I walked into our meeting room, I noticed another woman praying the rosary, before our group started. We pray the rosary as a group every month before class, but today was not one of those days. I went to help set up the coffee pot and put out the snack items. After about ten minutes, most of the women had arrived and the leader brought the group to attention.

We were currently reading the book *Walking with Mary* by Edward Sri that shows the life of the Mother of God as seen in the Bible. It takes the reader through the Blessed Mother's life as a woman who followed her path with faith and devotion, answering God's call. It was a strange coincidence that before the group leader chose this book for our class, I felt the need to get to know Mary better. I had never taken the time to study her life as the Mother of God. Over the years, I had prayed the rosary to her for help in times of stress but that was the extent of my time with her. As little girl, I had a small statue my mother bought for me of Mary and kept it in my bedroom. When I was about twelve years old, I remember visiting the large statue of Mary in the church courtyard and sometimes bringing flowers I picked to put at the base. The more I read in this book, the closer I felt to her as a person.

After about ten minutes into our small group discussion, I noticed a strange odor but didn't see anything. I looked around to see what could be the cause of this scent. It smelled like incense, the kind the church burns on certain holy days. There was no Mass being celebrated and it was not a holy day. Our class is held in the church basement. There was no one else in the lower level of the building. Other women noticed the scent as well so we all started talking about it. It was a strong odor of incense and it made me feel a little uneasy. We continued to smell the sweet scent of incense for the next hour.

Was this some kind of miracle? Everyone agreed that they smelled it and in the room of about twenty-five women, all had experienced this event.

Later, when I got home, I checked on the internet about the use of incense.

The sweet smell of incense and its rising smoke gave it a kind of natural symbolism. It became the image of something pleasing to God. The rising smoke came to symbolize a person's or people's prayers rising up to God. So in Psalm 141 we have the plea, "Let my prayer come like incense before you." (www.Americancatholic.org)

Early Christians also found symbolic meaning in incense. So too, had our ordinary Bible class. A group of women had been given a miracle, the scent of incense for the entire group to experience as a sign of God's presence.

3

Children of God

Except ye be converted, and become as little children,
ye shall not enter into the kingdom of heaven.

~ Matthew 18:3

†

Baby T

~ Janine Dates

BABY T WAS PLACED with amazing foster parents. As a Court
Appointed Special Advocate (CASA) for abused and neglected
children, I was assigned to Baby T. Baby T was taken into state
care on the day he was born because he tested positive for cocaine.

I scheduled my meeting when Baby T was only days old.
Wearing blue pajamas, I held him on my lap with his eyes closed.

"Well, I have to find out if this is where you should live and if
you are in a safe place," I said to Baby T.

Baby T responded with eyes closed and he gave me the
sweetest smile. "OK, I have my answer," I said. The foster parents
were so nervous not knowing what CASA does or if there was a
possibility Baby T would be taken from them.

The state's case was against the mother while the father was not
sure Baby T was his or not. The court ordered a paternity test, and
it took four months before the test revealed that he was indeed the
biological father.

There was no case against the father and legally the state was
required to turn over Baby T to his father immediately. The

caseworker called the foster parents and let them know she was on her way to pick up Baby T. The foster mom called crying her heart out and asked if there was anything that could be done.

I called the caseworker and asked that she not pick up Baby T and we would file a motion on Monday to keep the baby where he was until we could sort this out. The "father" had not spent any time with Baby T in past four months. The caseworker told me that legally they couldn't do that and the case was being transferred to another agency. The caseworker said, "Let me call you back."

A few minutes later she called and said, "OK, I suggested to Dad that we set up some visits to give him time to bond with the baby. He agreed. Off the record," she continued, "I don't believe he really wants Baby T and he shouldn't have him. You only have three weeks till court. Please find something to keep Baby T with these foster parents."

Four days later, the biological father's visit was set up.

The agency transported Baby T, and the dad picked up the mom for the visit. Just prior to the visit, the mother told me that Dad was smoking crack with someone on Tuesday. I just nodded, and the visit began. At the conclusion of the visit, Mom had Baby T bundled up and I casually said to Dad, "So, I hear you were smoking crack on Tuesday."

Dad jumped up and began yelling at the mom using the "F" word repeatedly. I took Baby T. "You stop right there—this child has *never* heard the 'F' word in his entire life, and it's not happening today," I said to the father.

The transporter and I hurriedly left the apartment. We heard a loud smack and knew Mom just got hit. I stayed long enough to make sure the transporter and Baby T were safely gone. Next the mom knocked on my car window and said, "It's true, I didn't lie to you."

"I know," I said.

Court day came, and I was able to include in my report that both parents' relationship was based on drugs and domestic violence. With that information, the judge ordered that both parents had to complete service plans and Baby T would stay in foster care. Neither parent successfully worked or completed the service plan.

At the end of October, the foster mom called and said Baby T was quite ill and having difficulty breathing. Foster mom was a pediatric intensive care nurse and had Baby T at the pediatrician's office. Both were stumped about what was causing the difficulty and the next stop was an ear, nose and throat specialist.

The appointment was Oct 27—what would have been our grandson's first birthday. I asked the foster mother to have the ENT doctor rule out laryngomalacia. Foster mom said that she and the pediatrician didn't think it was laryngomalacia. So I asked her to humor me and just ask the ENT doctor for me.

Stunned, the foster mother called me and said she could not believe it but Baby T had laryngomalacia. The treatment for laryngomalacia is typically the baby outgrows the condition, and in rare cases there is an out-patient procedure to correct the condition. Baby T had the procedure that day and was breathing easier.

I have no medical background whatsoever, and the foster mother asked me, "How did you know to ask?"

I explained our 6-month-old grandson, Baby D, suddenly died from laryngomalacia which is immature cartilage of the upper larynx that collapses inward during inhalation. The doctors told his parents that even if they had gotten to the emergency room, a doctor would specifically have to be looking for the condition.

I was grateful the foster mother asked the ENT to rule it out and have always felt Baby D was Baby T's angel and saved his life.

The foster mother and I still believe it was the hand of God that CASA was assigned to Baby T. If there had been no CASA, Baby T would be in a horrible situation with his biological father. We believe that God was present urging me to ask the foster mother to check out a condition I really know nothing about.

All this happened on what would have been our grandson's first birthday.

Strength When It Was Needed Most

~ Cinnamon Kettner

FEBRUARY 17TH, 2009.

This is a day that I will never forget. That was the day that my five-year-old son was diagnosed with an anaplastic astrocytoma of his brainstem, i.e. brain cancer. The doctor told us that Carter had 12 months to live. After two full days of crying and knowing that, for me, my life was changed forever, I prayed to God to grant my son these three things. I asked him, "Lord, please keep my son comfortable, happy and most of all fearless."

Little did I know that I was the one who really needed to be fearless. It was a grueling fifteen months that he hung on, facing every poke, every prod, every pill-popping, nauseating, throwing-up moment until there were tears in his eyes night, every PICC line access, every radiation session and chemo session and relentless stares and comments from seemingly cruel, but unknowing children. Yet, through it all he never stopped smiling. I know that strength was given to him for me.

Time seemed to pass slowly and for this I was extremely grateful. We were fortunate to be able to offer our beautiful boy many distractions to remind him that he was still a child and to give him such great joy, almost daily.

Through everything, I was the realistic parent who began mourning the day that we got the news. My husband, on the other hand, looked at the world through rose-colored glasses. He made hundreds of phone calls, sending our medical records and films all over the United States trying to find the one doctor on this great earth who would take my son's surgery case. This doctor did not exist. So, while I had already started mentally preparing to bury my baby, he had just given in to defeat and started to realize that this was an uphill battle that we could not win. By this time, I had already sought professional assistance and worked with a psychologist to help me sort out my feelings. This allowed me to be the staff and rod that my husband needed to lean on when his world hit that same wall that I had months before.

You know, they say that when such a tragedy hits home, a marriage will either fall apart or find the God-given strength to face even the most fierce opposition. I truly consider it such a blessing, that my husband Joe and I took turns finding the daily strength that we needed.

One day, closer to the end of his days here with us, on our way to another chemotherapy appointment, Carter said to me, "Mom, Jesus came to see me last night." He went on, "He told me that soon He was going to come back for me. He said that he was going to sprinkle magic fairy dust on me and that my wings were going to grow and that I was going to fly back to Heaven with Him." I sat and cried in the front seat, careful not to turn back, because I didn't want Carter to see my tears.

On May 12th, 2010, my son took his last breath here on earth. As tears run down my face, even now as I write this, I know my son is cancer free. I know he regained the ability to speak, the ability to walk and he is probably singing and jumping rope in heaven. For fifteen months, I prayed every day that God would keep my baby comfortable, happy and fearless. Not only were these three requests granted to me, but today I have a marriage that is as strong as it ever could be, and because Jesus came to Carter and told him that he would bring (him) back to heaven, I have absolutely no doubt in my mind that Heaven is for real and that one day we will all be reunited together forever, again.

A Life-Saving Night Visit

~ Rosemary Larson

IT WAS MY FATHER'S turn that night to sleep on the outside of the bed in the cramped bedroom of the cold-water flat. Named after my maternal grandmother, I was their first baby, Sara Sue, who slept in a small crib that abutted their iron bed, the crib slats up against the mattress. Poppa was sleeping on his side with his wrist wedged between the slats and his hand beneath my body to feel my movements during the night. He did so because he couldn't hear my cries and neither could my mother. They were deaf, profoundly deaf. In other words, he was as deaf as a person could be, a result of scarlet fever.

I loved them for seventy-five-plus years and their profound deafness was a constant. They never turned when I screamed, when the doorbell rang, a fire truck went by or when the screaming screech of the "el" trains made people wince. They communicated with signs, body language and facial expressions and had done so since they were two years old. None of their hearing siblings picked it up; they chose to write their messages. Their parents tried like heck and succeeded somewhat.

At this early time in their young relationship, which both their families ill-favored, my mother and father managed to get a license and marry. Poppa got a full-time job; Mama finished cooking and sewing classes for the deaf; and, they found a suitable and affordable flat. The families helped with hand-me-downs, groceries and automobile rides to anywhere that streetcars couldn't take them and plenty of unsolicited advice rode along. The whole of each family continued to be concerned and anxious for them but now the added responsibilities of a new baby were downright worrisome, the first pregnancy having ended in a miscarriage. They put themselves on heightened alert but mother was doing well nursing, diapering, bathing, taking temperatures, and along with Poppa, doting over me.

My mother was diligent about giving proof to her mother she was perfectly capable of living like a "hearie." She once caught Grandma sobbing in the old leather rocker. When my mother asked why she was upset, she signed, "I'm crying because you're deaf." Mother later said how much that upset her. "I was fine," my proud mother said, "And I am still fine."

This night, they climbed into bed as usual and Mama took the side next to the outside wall which was cold in the winter. The previous night, it was her turn to slip her small wrist in between the slats. Deep into the night, as Mama much later related, she was awakened by something shaking her toe, her right toe. Startled, her eyes opened to a tall, wispy, white, swirling figure standing at the foot of the bed that she immediately recognized. It was her mother. She said you could see through her.

Grandma had passed away just weeks before of heart trouble. She was dead. Mama knew she was dead and now, she was frozen in fear. "It was my mother," she signed in the retelling of the story

I had never heard. "I know my mother, and it was my mother but she wouldn't stop shaking my right toe, and she did it so hard and then disappeared." She recounted every detail and admitted at first, she thought it was a very real dream until she turned to see that Poppa was not in bed, the crib was pushed away, the blankets were askew and there was no Baby Sara.

Quickly, she got out of bed and walked through the bedroom door out into the living room and saw Poppa lying on the sofa, where he usually brought me when I was fussing in the night. I wasn't immediately noticed until Mama saw the top half of my body hanging out beneath Poppa's overturned body, my face wet from crying, my eyes fixed and I was turning blue. Poppa, who was not a small man, had rolled over on me.

Mama shoved him back then quickly pulled me out. She said she was so frightened and walked furiously back and forth "...a long time," she added, rubbing my back under my tear-soaked pajama top, hoping to shorten my quick deep sobbing, thinking of how to get an ambulance at that hour. She said it felt like I had quick hiccups that just wouldn't stop and my hair was so wet it looked glued to my head. She saw that I had been crying awhile.

Then I began to calm down, the sobbing stopped, my body relaxed and I wanted my thumb. It seemed like an hour, Mama said, but she saw that I was going to be OK. My father didn't awaken during the crisis, and my mother said it was because he was so tired from his job, hauling ashes all day. She put me back into the crib and said she leaned over it, put her hand on my back to make sure I was breathing. Then she began to cry and cry and cry, thinking about the first baby she had lost.

For years, she never shared that story. For years, her brothers, sisters and her father never knew. For years, even my father barely knew what happened, but from then on, Mama said her hands went through the slats every night and she told Poppa she would do it since he needed his sleep for work. Not until most of the family was gone did she tell me about the incident and said its memory still made her shiver: Her mother's warning, the near tragedy, and the timing of it all. Then, she signed simply, "There is no other explanation. It was my mother who saved you."

When to Take a Chance

~ Angelina

MY HUSBAND AND I are not gamblers but have gone once or twice a year to the local casino riverboat to try our luck at the slot machines.

One day we were driving by the gambling casino in Elgin, Illinois, and I had the urge to go in. We had not planned to go that day but something told me to go so my husband accommodated me and we stopped in. I spent my usual twenty dollars and was about to leave.

Suddenly, I spotted a little girl about three years old, standing by herself in the lobby. She looked nervous and scared. I went up to her and asked if she was lost. She said she was so I took her by the hand and said, "Come with me, and I can help you find your parents."

I looked around for a security guard but there were no guards in the area. I walked up to the gift shop and asked the clerk to call one for me, explaining the situation. She called security, and they put out a general announcement of a lost child in the lobby.

Shortly afterwards, two adults came to the gift shop and introduced themselves. They took the girl by the hand and left.

Afterwards, I realized why I got the urge to go gamble that day.

Where Do All the Babies Go?

~ Debra Kollar

"I WOULDN'T HAVE MUCH hope."

These were the words I remembered as I exited the automated doors at Rush Children's Hospital and into the sunlight after three days in a hospital room. I looked down at Interstate 90 past the hospital and the people zoomed past in their cars intent with getting through the morning commute. They were lost in daily happenings. I was at the door having my slow-motion moment: Those ill-fated days when a loved one dies, we lose a job, or some tragic event happens and time stops as we search around for some kind of meaning.

"I'll get the car," my husband said. His eyes were blood shot, his skin pallid, his back slightly bent from sleeping in a stiff reclining chair for too long.

As I waited for him, I had to fight the urge to go back. I was able to leave the confines of the hospital, feel the heat from an August sun on my face. My son, with his little curved fists, would never know what it was like to go out into the sunlight, to feel the wind wisp at his baby fine hair, feel a raindrop from an opening sky, or jump in a puddle of sticky mud afterward.

I was leaving a piece of me behind, down in that stainless steel morgue. I thought of him alone but I knew his soul had already left his body. It was traveling somewhere, maybe feeling the sunlight, feeling peace from the pain of being born without any lungs.

I had heard of many stories of infertility and miscarriage during my eight months of pregnancy. I was no different than anyone else. I didn't ask, "Why me?" There were plenty of women asking why me out there which showed me, it's not about something I did and it's not God's plan: It's biology and genetics and growth rate and sometimes, unexplainable.

The Bible is filled with verses for difficult times for a reason: We were never promised a perfect life. We were promised grace and healing, a way to get through difficulties with the knowledge that life has some kind of meaning even when bad things happen.

It has been several years since my son Sebastien died. Six months later, I was pregnant and I gave birth to a healthy boy, Noah. This is what God teaches us: We never forget our losses, this is life, but we can and do go on.

4

Angelic Visitors

*For he shall give his angels charge over thee,
to keep thee in all thy ways.*

~ Psalm 91:11

†

When to Listen with Your Heart

~ Deede Krage

I GREW UP ON forty acres, once part of a farm that had several barns, a creek and a pond which held an abundance of blue gill and cat fish and carp and the ever creepy craw fish. I lived with my parents and my Irish twin brother.

My grandparents, my mother's parents, lived next door, within calling distance. My brother and I essentially were raised and influenced by four people; family. Life was simple: Mind your parents and grandparents, do your chores without grumbling, say grace every day and remember your prayers before you go to bed.

Within the fabric of our lives on the forty acres, family and God were woven firmly into the fibers, we were taught they would always be with us and could always be counted on. My brother and I never questioned this, it just felt right. We also were taught we had our very own guardian angel, which watched over us and kept us safe.

Our Guardian Angel would also inform God if we misbehaved. I wasn't so sure if this were true or just something our parents would tell us so we would be good.

Between our houses was a fenced-in yard where my brother and I had a tire swing hung from an ancient elm tree that swung over our sand box. Every so often we would fill the sand box with water and pretend it was quick sand; the idea was to swing high over the sand box with one foot in the tire the other leg wrapped around it while holding tight to the rope and bellowing a Tarzan yell. Once past the quicksand we could jump to the safety of dry land avoiding death and of course any and all crocodiles that may be in the area. I'm sure that our angels got quite a kick out of this, and needless to say my brother and I never got hurt jumping off the swing or over the wooden sandbox.

I said this was *once* a farm. That's because my grandparents turned the acreage into a nine-hole, par-three golf course. Living along a golf course was great in the winter, but could be hazardous in the summer. All summer long we would need to be vigilant of the crack of the golf club shooting the small white ball like a missile down the first fairway, because we lived along that fairway. The aluminum siding on the east sides of both houses were pocked with dents from wayward golf balls, evidence that not all golfers shot straight and true to the green but tracked just left of the fairway into our back yards.

Some balls flew with such velocity that the dent they left on the houses were high up on the second level which meant they had an arc so high the ball could have landed in the front yard. Hence, the reason why our parents and grandparents fenced in the yard between the houses allotting my brother and me some protection from the sting of the small white balls that occasionally found their way into our games and our quicksand.

The west side our house was where Dad kept our small menagerie of animals, a large white rooster named Clybourn, a

MORE THAN A COINCIDENCE

Rhode Island Red hen named Red, a white duck named Daffy and one lone black-and-white rabbit named Josephine.

Every day, Dad would go into the pen to water and feed the animals. We were too young and Clybourn was too mean so only Dad was allowed in the pen.

One hot summer day, Dad was cleaning the animal pen and I was talking to him through the fence. It was quiet; barely a breeze whispered across your skin, the only sound was the soft clucking sound of the duck and chickens. I remember looking up at my dad. He had a rake in his hand, a white T-shirt and jeans he always wore when he worked in the yard. He was busy with his chores when I heard a very firm but gentle voice behind me say, "Pick up the hose."

I didn't hesitate; I squatted down and put my arms around a large coil of warm rubber hose laying in the grass at my feet, with my head down. I had just got a good grip on the hose when I heard CRACK!

One of the small white missiles hit the wooden fence just where my head had been when standing. I looked up and my Dad's face was ashen white. He saw I was all right and the ball had landed several feet from me, lying innocently in the dry late summer grass. He lowered his head and closed his eyes; I realize now he was giving a silent thanks to the Lord for keeping his little girl safe. He believed in God and our guardian angels. I know now he drew strength from his prayers and conversation with the Lord. He believed we were both spared that warm sunny afternoon.

After seeing my Dad's reaction, I looked behind me but there was no one to be seen. Turning to look only confirmed what I had already suspected, that my guardian angel had been right behind me, watching out for me just as my grandma and my parents had always told me he would. He was the one who asked me to pick up the hose; he had been the only one who saw the golf ball sailing right at me when neither my father nor I could see it or hear the fateful crack.

If it weren't for the faith that my parents instilled in both me and my brother, I'm not so sure I would have just obeyed the voice. If I had questioned it; turned to see who was speaking to me, or even hesitated for a breath of a moment the outcome of this story would have been very different.

Believe, let go and the Lord will lead you where you need to be when you need to be.

A Heavenly Presence

~ *Patrick J. Murphy III*

I FELT THE PRESENCE of someone or something in the car with me, but when I glanced back, the seat was empty.

I was driving back through Oklahoma to Texas, from visiting my grandparents in Chicago and dad and friends in Columbus, Ohio. In my arrogance, I had been driving for fifteen-plus straight hours. After a quick stop for gas and snacks, I returned to Interstate 35 when in the distance I saw a darkening cloud imminent of a coming storm.

A similar storm just two weeks prior sent me into a panic. My limbs shook and tears swelled in my eyes making me seek shelter from the road. I sat in my car for forty-five minutes barely able to breathe. My flight hormones were kicking into full gear; ever since I had wrecked my car two summers before outside of Tulsa, Oklahoma, in a storm that swept through the area, driving in rain terrified me. In that crash, I spun out hitting the guard rail twice. I was thankful I wasn't hurt and didn't hurt anyone in the process. There were close to sixty accidents that fateful day.

After that incident, I had trouble driving in bad weather and through Oklahoma. The coming storm I now faced scared me all over, but at two in the morning I didn't want to stop. I was tired, running on too much sugar and Red Bull to rationalize stopping. What could I do? I turned to God and prayed that He would see me home safely. As soon as I left the gas station, the feeling like I was being watched grew in the back of my mind.

Could someone have gotten into my car and was hiding? I didn't think this really could be possible since I religiously locked my doors. Several quick glances in the rearview mirror told me nothing but my luggage was there. Still, I had that queer the feeling. Then the storm came.

Lightening flashed and thunder rolled. My car shifted with the gusts of wind. I prayed like a mad man. The feeling of being watched sat with me like an unwelcome guest. Then as the clouds parted in front of me, the answers came to me.

The presence I felt in the car wasn't there to harm me, but instead to help me. The Lord had sent me a guardian angel to get me home. I knew I was going to be safe. Once I was through the storm, I said many prayers of thanks. My guardian angel saw me through the whole of the trip. I know that my faith is what got me through that day. I now have a guardian angel medal in my car, to remind me of that day and to always keep faith. I learned a valuable lesson that day: Through faith and prayer, God will lead the way.

Angels Among Us

~ Peg Ricketts

MY BROTHER-IN-LAW, RON—MY sister Cookie's husband—was a police officer. Ron's job at the time was called the "relief crew," filling in wherever he was needed across the city.

I was in a car accident and that evening, Ron was assigned to that area. He responded to the 911 call and came. He was afraid I was dead. My eyes were rolled back in my head. My torso was twisted so that my head was between the bucket seats. (I did have my seatbelt on.) He said my name and I opened my eyes and said "Ron, what are you doing here? Where are we?" He was able to call my husband and got permission to ride in the ambulance to the hospital with me.

Waking up in terrible pain, dizzy and disoriented, I realized I was in a hospital. A bit of comfort was recognizing this as the place I had delivered our four children. It was the middle of the night and I needed to go to the bathroom. Moving my head even a bit exacerbated the pain and dizziness. I started praying the Angel of God prayer.

*Angel of God, my guardian dear, to whom His love
commits thee here, ever this day be at my side, to light and
guard, to rule and guide. Amen."*

Suddenly a towering male nurse, dressed in white, came in the
room and tended to my needs. His golden hair and warm brown
eyes gave me serene peace. I dozed off and slept until I felt the sun
in the room. Still unable to move, I was relieved when a female
nurse came in. She explained I had been in a car accident the day
before. Having no memory of that, I took her word for it. As the
day went on, I asked if that male nurse was on duty again that
night. She said they didn't have any male nurses. She checked the
schedule and the float pool assuring me I must have been
dreaming or hallucinating. Because of the head injury I sustained,
having weird dreams became part of my "new normal" for some
time. Not wanting to, even though I believed I had met my
guardian angel, I kept his vision to myself and only talked to God
about it for some years.

As the years rolled on, my sister Rose was stricken with breast
cancer and began losing her long battle. Living in a small town, 400
miles from Omaha, she had frequently driven across Nebraska
from Alliance to Omaha for her treatments. As it became evident
the cancer was winning, hospice was called in and our sister
Cookie and her husband Ron took her in to their home. Rose's
husband and her six children were now making the journey as
often as they could. We kept vigil at her bedside for many weeks.

As her death approached, she became agitated and asked over
and over about the man watching her from the foot of her bed. She
floated in and out of consciousness, and I began to sense her vision
was as real as mine had been. When she was lucid, I asked her to

describe him. The details were just the same as I had recalled in my angelic encounter! Warmth flooded through me. I told her to ask him if he was her guardian angel. Murmuring, she drifted off. Peace and relaxation filled her beautiful face. Standing around her bed a few days later, she went home to her Heavenly Father.

For time away to meditate and pray, I often spend a few days and nights at a Benedictine Retreat Center about an hour away from home. Father Anselm Gruen, a saintly Benedictine priest from Germany, who has written many books on angels, came to the Retreat Center in Schuyler and gave a weekend presentation when I was there. At one point, he asked if any of us had a story to share. My hand shot up and after telling my story, I asked if Rose and I could have the same guardian angel.

All things are possible with God, he said.

The manifestation to her may have been to put my mind and heart at ease about my experience, and, at the same time, confidence in Our Lord's presence during her cancer battle.

5

Still Small Voice

Trust in the Lord with all thine heart;
and lean not unto thine own understanding.

~ Proverbs 3:5

†

A Whispered Command

~ *Suzi Sandoval*

I DECLINED SUPPER FRIDAY night since I felt nauseous. Instead, I bid the family good night and went to bed. When I awoke the next morning, Saturday, December 23, 2007, the aroma of coffee set my stomach to churning. Light-headed, I tottered to the bathroom. I didn't have time to position myself over the toilet bowl when the volcano in my stomach violently erupted, spewing blood on the wall behind the toilet. I braced myself against the wall as the next blood explosion assailed the wall once again; then the final upheaval—this time finding its mark in the toilet.

My daughter, a nuclear medicine tech surveyed what now resembled a slaughterhouse and sprang into action. She communicated the situation to the 911 operator all the while calmly giving instructions to the other adults in the house. Despite the wind, icy roads and a thirty-car pileup on Interstate 40, paramedics swiftly responded.

In the emergency room, the momentum picked up as human hands worked diligently to stop the bleeding from ruptured varices in my esophagus. As tubes pushed up my nose and down my throat, and IVs hit and miss assailed my body, I prayed, *the Lord is my Shepherd, I shall not want.*

Suddenly a peaceful light embraced me, carrying me beyond the recognizable dimensions of the earth. It released me from a web of misery into vast nothingness. While the doctors and medical staff continued their life-saving mission on my traumatized body I journeyed further into brilliance. The radiance filled the immense emptiness. Released from the shackles of my earthly flesh, I sank into its pearly beauty. I transformed into a resplendent creation. Elated, I floated aimlessly and alone through absolute silence. How could such an unfamiliar place seem so right? I drifted through the light enjoying peace and comfort. The solitude refreshed me.

I heard subtle breathing. I was no longer alone. "Who?" I wondered. I didn't see anyone, but I felt someone. Then the subtle breath whispered to me in a voice unrecognizable — without earthly qualities. So graceful, so smooth, so impassioned, this burning voice. The voice consumed my entire being. My ears served no purpose.

"Breathe," it gently commanded.

I obeyed. I took a breath and when I did, the light began to fade like the setting sun. "Don't go," I tried to speak, but the tube in my throat prevented me from uttering a word.

Pain and discomfort attacked my body as the glow surrounding me faded into obscurity. I desired the soothing light, for it removed me from all suffering. Mystified by the astonishing encounter, I knew that no matter which way things went, I would be all right — with God, everything ends well.

The discord of the medical staff and the blinding fluorescence of the emergency room punished my throbbing head. Shadows moved about. The hazy apparition at the foot of ER gurney came into focus. My three daughters huddled together. Grief etched their faces. My ears functioned again.

The doctor's agitated voice barked commands, "Why isn't that transfusion started?"

"We're trying to stabilizer her," an apprehensive voice replied.

"You can't stabilize her without blood. Get the line started!" the doctor growled.

Such insignificant quibbling annoyed me. My surroundings served as an obstacle to a place that felt free of pessimism, discontentment and pain. My inability to regain access to the peaceful light added to my agitation. I didn't belong to this chaos; I belonged to the blissful brilliance. It filled me with love and overwhelming joy. But like a water mirage in the desert it had disappeared, leaving me thirsty for more.

Like the gentle ebb of the ocean my strength returned as Psalm 118:17 flowed through my veins.

I will not die but live and will proclaim what the Lord has done (NIV).

I now have a plan for the rest of my life—a testimony of hope to share with those in need of comfort.

"Things happen for a reason." This mantra is overused but effective in explaining what humans can't comprehend. Saturday morning, December 23, 2007 happened for a reason. What began as a chaotic, life-threatening day quickly shifted into a glorious and unforgettable experience.

Did I make it to heaven? Perhaps I journeyed to the portal of God's heavenly home. I didn't hear cymbals and trumpets or angels' singing praises announcing my arrival. I believe God reserves that for those actually entering his kingdom. He did allow me to taste the promised joy of the resurrection. There is life after death. It's full of comfort and joy and love

Author's postscript: "I'm more than a survivor, I'm a thriver." It started at age sixteen when a drunk driver set off a chain of events that changed her life forever. The life-saving blood given to her the night of her car accident unknowingly infected her with hepatitis C. In 2001, Suzi's doctors declared she would not see another birthday. The hepatitis had destroyed her liver. She put this catastrophe in God's hands. Her prayers were answered in 2002 at the University of Colorado Hospital in Denver where she received a second chance at life through a liver transplant.

Follow Your Heart

~ *Jennifer Burgsteiner*

IN SEPTEMBER 2008, I contemplated attending a Christ Renews His Parish weekend at my church. At the time, I did not realize this spiritual retreat was based on the Word of God with prayer, scripture, liturgy, and sharing. I was unsure whether to attend the weekend as I am one of those people that need to gather as much information as possible before I make a decision.

I called the number in the bulletin to see if I could get some more information. Much to my chagrin, the woman on the other line was unspecific as to what the weekend entailed. She mentioned the weekend would be relaxing and just to "come and let the Holy Spirit be with me."

In the past if someone mentioned "the Holy Spirit," I got a little freaked out. It was not every day that the people in my life used the words like *Holy Spirit* in their daily vocabulary let alone mentioned *God.* I hung up the phone and pondered whether to attend the retreat. I told my husband what the woman said about the Holy Spirit and my growing skepticism. I decided I would attend as I had nothing to lose and maybe the Holy Spirit had something to say to me. I figured at a minimum the weekend would give me time to focus and think some things through as I was laid off my job a few months prior.

I was devastated, bitter and angry when I decided to take the severance package and quit my job. I turned down a move out of state so as not to uproot my family and cause my husband to find a new job. I was just getting the hang of the mom-wife-career-woman balancing act after going back to work after the birth of my children. I saw my job as my ticket to temporary motherhood freedom and back to the adult world with real conversations and no one to worry about but myself. As an overachiever, I had never been let go of a job and I was not ready to end this chapter of my life. I was told by many that my situation was a blessing in disguise; although I did not feel that way at the time.

Consider it all joy, my brothers, when you encounter
various trials, for you know that the testing of your faith
produces perseverance. ~ James 1:2-3

It seemed a contradiction to be so obsessed about my job as an accountant but I had worked hard for my CPA and had a good reputation. At the same time, I had two three-year-old twins at home to raise. I would always have my CPA but they were only young once. They were truly a gift from God, a gift I had personally asked for many years ago.

I remembered that day in high school after watching a set of twins with my best friend, when I told her it would be great to have twins of my own when I was married. To this she said that I was crazy as babysitting twins is probably easier than raising them.

Fast forward to a few years after I was married and my husband and I were trying to conceive. We tried for a year and then went to a fertility expert to find out I had a fertility problem. I had laparoscopic surgery to remove the scar tissue that was blocking my reproductive organs. We were very excited that we could still conceive and the doctor encouraged us to start trying as soon as possible. We were successful in conception, but he failed to mention the risk of a multiple birth. At my twelfth week of pregnancy, a blood test revealed my hormone levels were extremely high and an ultrasound showed us two heartbeats; we were having the twins that I prayed for. I shared the great news with my best friend who said I should have been careful what to wish for as He may just fulfill your wish.

> And the people were bringing children to him that he might touch them, but the disciples rebuked him. When Jesus saw this he became indignant and said to them, "Let the children come to me; do not prevent them for the kingdom of God belongs to such as these." ~ Mark 10:13-14

During my Christ Renews His Parish weekend, I asked the Holy Spirit for direction about my decision to raise my children (the twins God gave to me) or take another accounting job. He provided me with divine guidance as to the direction of my priorities, and I decided to stay at home as that was the best decision for my family. My love for home is different than my love for my accounting job. The rewards and benefits of staying home are not paid like my accounting jobs in a monetary value, and I have to be patient as the fruits of my labor will not be known for years to come. God made it very clear that despite my selfish desires to pursue my own will, I needed to follow His will and I pay more attention to the relationships that I have neglected in the past including the one I have with Him.

> *For we ourselves were once foolish, disobedient, deluded, slaves to various desires and pleasures, living in malice and envy, hateful of ourselves and hating one another. But when the kindness and generous love of God our savior appeared, not because of righteous deeds we had done, but because of his mercy, he saved us through the bath of rebirth and renewal by the Holy Spirit.* ~ Titus 3:3-5

The Holy Spirit has helped renew and restore my relationship with God. Instead of attending church every Sunday, just to attend; I listen with an open heart and mind for the Holy Spirit's message for me. I now put my life in God's hands so that He can mold and shape it according to His will and not mine.

> *Yet, O LORD, you are our Father; we are the clay and you the potter: we are all the work of your hands.) May the Holy Spirit be with you!* ~ Isaiah 64:7

Life as a Spiritual Quest

~ Julie Ostrow

WONDERING IF THERE IS *a spiritual life or entity out there?*

I wasn't necessarily on a quest to find my spiritual life but I recall feeling and knowing that if I ever found my spiritual home, I would know it.

I was living in the city of Chicago climbing the corporate ladder and doing what I "was supposed to" be doing with my life. Yet, every so often, I would get a twinge in my soul nudging me to do something else with my life. What would it be? When I got that twinge, I knew I would do something with my life that involved sharing my creativity, my personality, and my humor to help others improve their lives. But, what would that be? What would it look like?

Once I got the twinge for a better life, I would do my research about various careers that would meet my needs to be me and help others—speech pathology, music therapy, art therapy, kindergarten teacher. But, I would get scared. I would request information packets from area schools and programs but the twinge for being me would die down by the time I received the packet of information in the mail. So I continued on with my corporate life.

The twinge never went away.

I believe that there is a dream on my heart that was placed there by God, Angels, Spirit, or perhaps even my deceased relatives.

As I continued on my corporate career path, it seems I became unhappy with what I was doing—or not doing—with my life.

As I look back on my life, I realize that "twinge" was my God, Angels, Spirit, or perhaps even my deceased relatives guiding me.

There were spiritual twinges all along the way. I would acknowledge those twinges, yet, I wouldn't act on them. Instead, I discounted them because I thought they came from me. This is where I can share that I wasn't always a confident person. I doubted everything I did. I was afraid of making a mistake, and, worse, being judged, especially by family members. Although the judgment and criticism that came from family members most likely came from a loving, helpful place, I still took judgments as criticisms and attacks on my character and who I was. So, when I heard—or felt—a great idea from Spirit, I fell into my habit of discounting ideas that would come to me.

When did I start listening—truly listening—to Spirit?

Enough was enough. How long was I going to choose to be miserable climbing the corporate ladder and becoming someone who I was not?

The parents of a friend of mine from college who were like a second set of parents to me (I'll call them Mr. and Mrs. T) had planted the seed of moving back to North Carolina, and if I did, I could stay with them for a while. (I had gone to North Carolina State University in Raleigh, N.C., and, while there, my friend and a group of us would take regular weekend trips to the beach, where my "second set of parents" lived.)

A twinge planted by humans

When Mrs. T suggested I could live with them, I said, "Thank you so much" but thought, "Nope. I'm on the fast track of my corporate career. I'm not moving to the sleepy town of Wilmington, N.C."

Well, fast forward to about four years later when I had had enough of the corporate world. I remembered my friend's parents' offer to live with them for a while. I believe that seed that was planted years earlier was another spiritual twinge. I called my friend and asked if the offer still stood. Thankfully, it did.

And the stars aligned

As I made the decision to go on sabbatical from the corporate world, I continued to receive signs and affirmations that I had, indeed, made the right decision.

Money. A week after I made the decision to leave my job as a marketing manager at a pharmaceutical company, we managers received notices that we would be receiving management bonuses from the previous quarter.

Job. My friend in North Carolina had lined up a job as a hostess at a new restaurant in town.

Subletting my apartment. How smart is it to move out of state with an apartment you still have a lease on? I don't actually remember how I found the person who would sublet my apartment but I do remember he paid for the three months in full.

As these signs continued to appear, I continued to feel more and more secure and happy about my decision to leave the big city and live in a small southern town for a while. I would be taken care of. I was doing the right thing.

The first of many signs

As I drove down the highway on my way to North Carolina, I realized my bike rack was not holding my bike very securely. As I began to slow down and try to come up with a solution, I thought, "I need something to hold this bike down ... like more bungee cords." I pulled off to the side of the road to see if I could figure out a way to fasten the bike more securely with whatever I had in my car.

I would say it was within ten minutes in what seemed to be out of nowhere, an IDOT (Illinois Department of Illinois) truck appeared. At first, I was a little hesitant with two men approaching my car. As they approached my car, they were holding several industrial strength bungee cords. "Hey, we found these on the side of the road and thought you might need these."

A sense of relief and gratitude filled my heart.

As I got back into my car, I took a deep breath and smiled. I heard, "You are meant to go on this adventure to North Carolina. You will be safe. You will be taken care of."

The sign of all signs

My trip to North Carolina included a stop in Cincinnati to spend time with some college friends. By the time I reached Cincinnati, it was in the middle of the night. Have you ever driven the beltline around Cincinnati? It is a bit challenging. Add a tired driver who's never driven it. Grr.

So, I pulled off into the parking lot of a country store to look at the map and figure out how to get where I needed to go. (Note: This was long before GPS.)

As I was figuring out the map, a truck pulled into the parking lot. I thought, "Great. I'm going to get killed here and no one will know what happened to me. I am a single woman sitting in the parking lot of a store off the beaten path in the middle of the night." Just then, a woman got out of the truck with a stack of that day's newspaper and dropped them off on the porch of the store.

As the woman was walking past my car to her truck, she paused, turned around, and smiled at me and simply said, "God bless."

I felt relieved and at peace.

That would be one of many times where I *felt* the knowing of being taken care of and being on the right path.

Synchronicity

So why did I really move to Wilmington, N.C.? Did I need a sabbatical from the corporate world? To find myself ? To just relax? To find God?

The answer: Yes.

I found myself. I found that my Self was with me all along.

I found a spiritual community by how I like to call synchronistic steps and occurrences.

Here they are...

I walked with coffee to a bookstore and saw a sign in the store for a metaphysical book club meeting. I attended the book club meeting and met a Reiki practitioner named Joy. Joy told me during the Reiki session that she "heard" that she was to tell me of the church community that I would click with. She said, "Go to Unity Christ Church of Wilmington."

When I walked into the Unity Christ Church of Wilmington, I cried. I cried every time I went there for the next month. I had found my spiritual home. In finding this spiritual home, I found a community that embraced my humor, creativity, and ability to make others laugh. Revisiting the thought of not being good enough, I had the continuous thought that "if I can make people laugh, so can everyone else. It's no big deal." That is not true. My church community and spiritual friends lifted me up as someone with a spiritually guided gift. I eventually learned to embrace my gift and have the confidence to share it with others. I performed stand-up comedy for the first of many times. It was at Unity Christ Church of Wilmington, where I led my very first humor and laughter workshop. That was 2001.

So I launched my "Find The Funny Enterprises" business where I aimed to share my gift with others.

Talk about embracing who I am! I won the first ever American Laughing Championship held in conjunction with the annual conference of the Association for Applied and Therapeutic Humor (AATH). Through the years, when people would hear my laugh, I was either complimented or criticized. Then, I would listen more to the criticism rather than the compliments. Now, I gravitate toward positive people who embrace joy. During the 2013 laughing championship, I fully embraced being enveloped in love and laughter from my humor and laughter community of AATH.

I am now thriving as the Humor, Laughter, and Improv coach where I confidently coach groups and organizations to embrace their humor and laughter in addition to helping them develop their ability to be in the moment and think on their feet. I help them use those skills to improve their lives and their interactions and relationships with others. I believe that by having listened to those initial "spiritual twinges," I am on the path I was seeking so long ago.

Tests of Faith

~ Constance P.

MY HUSBAND HAD TO have some medical tests before his upcoming knee replacement surgery. He had been limping for more than five years and had shortness of breath. He kept putting off the surgery until finally he agreed to do it.

I had a feeling that he would not pass the heart tests. The stress test and echocardiogram showed problems and he was ordered to have an angiogram. I was worried about the complications such as bleeding, heart attack, stroke and death. Even though it is uncommon, this was the first time he was having this procedure and as a diabetic, he was at greater risk for all of these.

I was in the room with the doctor as he discussed the outcome of the angiogram with my husband. One artery was so damaged and closed up he could do nothing for it. He put a stent in another artery. A stent is a small stainless steel mesh tube that is placed by a catheter and permanently embedded within the artery wall to prop the artery open, preventing it from collapsing.

Trying not to worry, I was driving to work when I heard a voice say to me. "Oh, ye of little faith!"

Was that my own inner voice telling me to calm down or something else?

As a Catholic who is still on the journey of getting closer to Jesus, who has worked on her faith through Bible classes and sharing her beliefs with others, I think I know the answer.

By the way, my husband's angiogram went well as did the knee replacement surgery my husband had the following week!

6

Not Alone

Peace I leave with you, my peace I give unto you:
not as the world giveth, give I unto you. Let not your heart
be troubled, neither let it be afraid.

~ John 14:27

✝

Junction Angel

~ Leticia Rivera Davis

I LIVED IN COLORADO Springs for twelve years before I moved to Kennesaw, Georgia—a suburb just northwest of bustling Atlanta. Atlanta is infamous for its drivers' habits and its traffic. To me, the traffic in Atlanta is so stressful; driving in it is one of my least favorite things to do.

Driving here is even more stressful when you are unfamiliar with the area. As a new arrival, I always avoided was commonly known as "Spaghetti Junction." It is an intersection of Interstates 85 and 285 and a massively intertwined traffic interchange—five-level stack—just northeast of Atlanta. From an aerial view, it resembles a plate of spaghetti, piled high.

One warm Sunday afternoon, I was headed to the house of a friend who lives in the northeast suburb of Norcross. This was my very first time visiting. I had a printed copy of the Google Maps instructions to help me navigate the unfamiliar roads. It indicated that the best and fastest route between her house and mine was, you guessed it—Spaghetti Junction!

I was panicky, driving my little Honda Civic on the interstate, and when I finally approached the junction, I suddenly heard a loud bang. At first, I dismissed the noise as simply something that hit my car. Normally, I would have stopped the car to inspect the damage but the traffic was so heavy I decided to wait until I cleared the junction. As the road ahead ascended, I continued to drive in the left lane anticipating a merge ahead. Then I started to hear a loud and repetitive thumping noise. For a moment, I thought something was falling off the car. I did not fathom what was really causing that awful noise. As I was driving the car on the crest of the junction, suddenly, a man driving an old beat-up truck on the passenger side of my car caught my attention. He made a circular motion with his finger and pointed to the back of my car. Yep! I had a flat tire.

As I slowly veered my car to the right, I could see the traffic behind me increasing, and the faces of the angry drivers. I grew increasingly nervous and scared. The traffic then descended on the interchange as I slowly made my way to the right side of the road. I carefully cut in front of cars trying to looking for a safe place to pull over. When I finally found a spot to stop, I noticed that it was very close to the connecting highway. I came to a complete stop on the side of the road, and parked in a confined space between the merging descending traffic and a concrete ramp divider. It was too close for comfort.

After turning off the ignition, I prayed, "Lord, please help me. I wish my dad had taught me how to change a tire. What do I do now?" Sure, I took a Powder Puff class once, but I've never changed one alone.

I started feeling desperate. The car rested in a dangerous position. Cars were flying down the highway and zipping by me. I quickly discovered that I was unable to exit the car from the driver's side. In fact, the cars were whipping past me so fast and close that my car vibrated. I decided to get out of the car on the passenger's side where I had enough room to open the door and safely step out to check the damage.

Surprisingly, on the other side of the ramp, I saw the man from the beat-up truck again. He had parked and waited for me to exit my car. It was hard to hear over the traffic noise but he asked me if I spoke Spanish. "Sí, Señor!" I answered loudly in our native language. He then asked me if I needed help. Once again, I answered with an affirmative. He quickly ordered me to put the hazard lights on and open the trunk of the car. Very grateful for his help, I did so dutifully. I quickly reached in the car and pushed the buttons on the console that made it happen. When I looked at him again, the angelic man had already jumped over the ramp and was quickly removed the jack out of the trunk. He had the car cranked up in no time.

As he took off the lug nuts off the blown out tire, he confessed to me that he was a mechanic and had recently moved south from Chicago with his family. I thanked God for his relocation. I was thankful for the kindness of an absolute stranger who came to my rescue. We shared stories about our families and our relocations to Atlanta while he single-handedly removed the blown tire from the car. We continued our conversation as he diligently replaced it with the emergency spare tire. He mentioned that he had a throat cancer operation and left his old city to start a new life near his family in Atlanta.

"I'm grateful to have made it this far," he commented. Indeed, a closer look at him revealed his disfigured chin and neck. I felt like we were no longer strangers.

As he finished tightening the remaining lug nuts on the newly mounted tire, I thanked him for helping me once again. I introduced myself and shared only my first name — Leticia. He said his name was George Rivera. Suddenly, a chill entered my body like a current of energy. He had the same name as my deceased *father.* My guardian angel came to my rescue as a mechanic with my father's name!

"Oh my God! That's my father's name!" I exclaimed excitedly at him. He flashed a warm smile.

What are the odds of having a mechanic with the same *exact* name as my father stop on a *busy* junction to help me? A small part of me wondered if there could be a logical explanation. I asked myself, was this divine intervention or just a happy coincidence? Angels and divine intervention have always intrigued me. My life has always had a consistent flow of little happenstances and signs I did not understand. This time, I chose to rationalize the event as a spiritual encounter and validation that my father had indeed connected to me.

As a child, my life was not always so easy. Growing up, I could not always depend on my father. As his first child, I always wanted a close relationship with him, but he had difficulty expressing his feelings. He had a closer relationship with my brother. My two sisters and I felt cheated. I never once heard him tell me that he loved or was proud of me However, when money was tight, he always made sure we had a roof over our heads. Mom always made sure we had plenty to eat, good grades and decent clothes to wear. I remembered that my father once worked in a gas station with a tire repair service. Later on, my parents separated then divorced but reconciled. He suffered from diabetes and became a double amputee. My father passed away after a stroke. After my father's death, I was heartbroken. I never once heard him tell me that he loved or was proud of me. Since my father's death, I have received many messages from him that confirmed that he truly did love me. I also found letters he had written affirming his love, faith and hopes.

When George the mechanic finally put away the jack and closed the car trunk, I gave him a warm hug and said, "Thank you so much for stopping to help me. I don't know what I would've done without you. You have been a guardian angel to me."

"We should all be guardian angels to one another," he responded.

I agreed wholeheartedly. With that said, I vowed to be more concerned with what I can do for others. It is a lesson I learned from my junction angel.

It was all so surreal. Before parting, he gave me a business card with his name and telephone number scratched on the back of it. We exchanged goodbyes, and I went on my way in amazement. Shortly thereafter, I strategically placed his card on my car's sun visor. To this day, it remains there. Every time I glance at it, I think about my divine mechanic and pray that he remains wonderfully blessed with health and happiness. I also thank both of my fathers in heaven for continuously watching over me.

Most importantly, after our encounter, my faith strengthened. I am convinced that the unseen forces of the spiritual world have the means to intervene in certain events. I know, too, that my father's spirit remains connected to me still, even though I may not see him. Pay attention, dear reader! You, too, may cross paths with strangers who serve a higher purpose—sending messages from the afterlife. Sometimes, they may even come with a familiar name!

Nancy and Joe—a Love Story

~ Nancy C.

WE GREW UP TOGETHER in 1940 on the northwest side of Chicago and went to the same elementary school. We lived a block apart. After school, we went our separate ways as we grew older, met and married other spouses and lived our own lives. We didn't meet again for fifty years.

In 1990, on July 20, I moved back to Chicago alone. Unbeknownst to me at the time, Joe's wife passed away the following week.

In December 1990, there was a fifty-year grammar school reunion where Joe and I met. We were both so excited and happy to see each other and spend the whole evening with all our friends.

Right then and there, I felt God had a plan for us.

Three months later, Joe called and asked if I had any coffee. He came over and spent the whole day trying to catch up on everything. We started to date and our courtship lasted three years, and we fell in love. My family was ecstatic but Joe's three daughters did not share our joy.

In 1993, he proposed, and at age sixty-five we were married in 1995 at church and had a beautiful reception. I felt so bad for Joe that his family would not give us their blessings but that was their choice.

The first ten years were such a blessing for both of us to be together. Joe was so good hearted and loving, having friends, neighbors and family around for barbeques and holidays.

In 2004, things started to change. Joe started to cough and he lost forty pounds. After a few visits to Loyola Medical Center, Joe was diagnosed with three spurs in his throat. He had a tracheotomy put in his throat and a feeding tube in his stomach. I became his full-time caregiver for the next seven years, which necessitated my training in how to care for my Joe.

Many health issues followed such as urinary tract infections and ulcers in his back. He became incontinent and needed a catheter which needed to be cleaned daily. At night I would cry for what my poor Joe was going through. I asked God to give me the strength and energy I needed every day.

Then Joe had heart failure which resulted in his getting a pacemaker.

In 2013, I found blood in my urine and the biopsy showed a cancerous tumor in my bladder. The surgery was successful, thank God, but it left me no energy to care for Joe and lift him in and out of his wheelchair. My doctors advised me to make other arrangements for Joe's care so I did.

I found a good health center where Joe would have care around the clock. In August 2013, Joe began to live at Tower Hill Health Care Center with physical, occupational and speech therapy. It was also close to Joe's doctors and hospital. For the first few months, Joe was holding his own, but he would drift off and lose his concentration—the start of dementia. I prayed all the time to help Joe and asked Jesus to please help me during this stress.

Joe developed high temperatures, very low blood pressure and couldn't breathe, so he went back to the hospital for seven days on antibiotics, oxygen and irrigation of his lungs. Nothing was helping and his body and his organs were shutting down. After doctors spoke to me, Joe went back to Tower Hill under Hospice. I sat and held his hand, kissed his face and prayed the Good Lord end his battle of seven years. No one should have to suffer like my Joe did. On Saturday, July 5, 2014 at 10:50 p.m., the good Lord embraced my Joe and ended his hell on earth.

Jesus Christ is my constant companion. Without Him, I never could have made it. Now I live with my memories and gratitude! Thank God for your blessings. You gave Joe back to me after fifty years....

"For every sorrow, pain and ache, Jesus will never forsake.
Thank you, sweet Jesus."

Nina's Story

~ Nina F.

I WAS ON MY way to work as a server at a local restaurant. It was the day after Thanksgiving and the weather was misty out. The roads became slippery and my car started to fishtail. I soon lost control and hit a light pole. Finally, my car started to roll over.

All the while, I kept hearing a voice that sounded like my grandmother's voice. It said, "You'll be fine. You'll be OK. Help is on the way."

The car rolled over, landed upside down and on the other side of the highway. My air bag had deployed, and I realized I was stuck upside down in my car. I unbuckled my seat belt, and later remember sitting outside of the car. I had crawled but it felt like someone pulled me out of the smashed windshield to safety. I felt my grandmother was there, and I looked around but did not see anyone.

Two cars stopped to give help. It turns out the different drivers were off-duty paramedics and came to my aid. (What are the chances of that happening?) One of them called my parents and explained I was in a car accident but was OK. They worked together on me and soon an ambulance came. I told the ambulance driver I had Christmas presents in the car and asked if they could take them. It was against policy but they did it anyway. Otherwise who knows what would have happened to them after the car was towed?

At the hospital, I was sitting on the table when a nurse came in the room. She said, "I think I am in the wrong room because there is supposed to be a person from a car accident in this room."

I told her I was in the car accident and just got here. Apparently my injuries were so minor, she couldn't believe I was the victim. At the time, all I had were a few scratches on my hand and a black eye.

The nurse turned white and ran out of the room. Another nurse came in shortly afterwards. She apologized for the previous nurse running out of the room and explained she is retiring soon and apparently was in shock. She said to me, "You are blessed. You should have been in major surgery, with the type of accident you had. Your car was totaled and your injuries should have been much worse."

When I got home, all I had was some little flecks of glass in my hair that my sister helped take out, the black eye and the small cuts on my hand. I really believe my guardian angels protected me throughout the whole ordeal.

My grandmother and I were close when I was young and although she is passed away, I still talk to her in my dreams. I feel a special connection with her and am grateful for her presence at a time when I really needed help.

Looking Down from Heaven

~ Monica Lee

GOD WORKS IN MYSTERIOUS ways, and some small so-called coincidences can bring a bounty of comfort.

My little brother Curt died at age 26 in a weather-related highway crash. He was on his way home from watching a Vikings play-off game with friends in northern Minnesota, and it was snowy and blowing, as it often is near Fargo, North Dakota. In the flurries, he accidently crossed the center line and hit another car head-on. The other car ended up in the ditch; Curt's Bronco ended up in the middle of the road with him still inside. In the poor visibility, a semi-truck then hit Curt's car. He died at the hospital a couple hours later.

That was more than 16 years ago. It was a terrible, terrible shock at the time. It is the only grief I have ever felt physically, besides emotionally.

I still miss him and the relationship we might have had if he were still alive. But I think of him often in common circumstances haloed with strange synchronicity:

- My nephew, Drew, was conceived very close to the time my brother died. Drew — a joy to our family — was born nine months later, and his middle name is Curtis.
- My sister's second son Logan was born on Aug. 4, Curt's birthday.
- My sister's third son Breck shares his status with my brother, also third in birth order. Both Curt's and Breck's conceptions were surprises.

The new family I formed when I met and married my second husband has Curt coincidences, too.

I thought of my brother often one recent summer when I was spending every weekend at the stock car races near DeKalb, Illinois; my husband and his brother relived their glory days racing around a dirt track and attempting to be the last junker standing in the nightly demolition derbies. Curt was a gear head who studied to be a car mechanic. Curt would have loved the stock car races, and my devotion to my husband's weekly races that summer not only made me feel that Curt was around me but fostered an even better relationship between me and the man who's not my brother, but like a brother — my brother-in-law, Ted.

Even more meaningful moments center around my stepson, Caswell, whom I met for the first time when he was 12. Curt was 12 when I left home to go to college. As I dated my now-husband and contemplated stepmothering Caswell, I felt like God was giving me a second chance to form a relationship with a 12-year-old boy. Oddly, Caswell shares Curt's initials: CW.

My stepson's teenage antics often remind me of my brother, whose mirthful sense of humor was one of his best characteristics. When he was a little boy, he had learned to appreciate poetry and humor from our droll grandfather, but he hadn't yet learned the finer points. Just the *way* he told a joke was the funniest part. As he told the joke, the suspense wasn't in the punch line but whether he would have one or if he did, how he would botch it.

"Knock, knock."

"Who's there?"

"Three pigs."

"Three pigs who?"

"Knock knock."

"What? I don't get it," I'd said. "'Knock knock' is the pigs' last name? That doesn't make any sense."

"They're knocking. That's the joke. They're not ringing the doorbell."

"Oh, Curt, they're not ringing the doorbell. *That's* the joke. The last line should be 'Three pigs who can't reach the doorbell.'"

"Oh." And then he would laugh like it was the funniest joke he'd ever told.

One recent Christmas, I heard Bob & Doug McKenzie's version of the "12 Days of Christmas." This dumb song from 1982 is the perfect mix of the 1980s, up-north humor and backwoods hicks that come together in the perfect union of Curt memories. He was all that: A kind soul with a goofy sense of teen-age humor and a love of snowmobiling (and, on the first day of Christmas, maybe even a beer … in a tree). I played the YouTube video for teenage Caswell, who found it hilarious.

I know Curt would have adored Caswell as much as I do. I am grateful God gave me this gift of my brother for a short time and now the gift of my stepson as well.

On a recent Jan. 17, the anniversary of my brother's death, another Curt coincidence occurred. He wouldn't want me and my family continuing to dwell in sorrow on the January day. The date now has a new significance. Our family celebrated another new baby when my cousin's daughter Karletta was born.

Coincidence? Possibly. Strange occurrences happen all the time, and we choose to assign meaning to these events. I can feel my brother looking down and smiling on me. It's as if we are still connected through the family.

God's ways of soothing grief are priceless.

7

Words of God

*To every thing there is a season, and a time
to every purpose under the heaven.*

~ Ecclesiastes 3:1

†

Keep Calm and Stay Strong

~ Madeline K.

MY BROTHER CALLED TO tell me that my father could no longer swallow and was put on hospice. For the past year, he had been fed pureed foods and due to his Alzheimer's disease, often choked or ingested some of the food. He had been on hospice once before, about a year ago when he got pneumonia.

When Dad first entered the nursing home six years ago, he was able to walk, talk, feed and dress himself. He could recognize some family members and enjoyed reading and watching TV. Gradually, he became weaker physically and mentally as the disease progressed. For the past year, he was in a wheelchair and could try to say a few words but now, at age 89, it seemed like it was his time to go.

I had heard other residents who had stopped eating died after about a week and was concerned. He was only on oxygen and morphine. Since he retired to live in Arizona, I visited him twice a year. I needed to book a flight as I lived 1,400 miles away from Dad. There were six of us siblings who all live out of state and we started to make plans. I worried, thinking *would I make it on time?*

How soon should I leave? The worry became nerve wracking so I went to the mall to distract myself.

In the first department store I entered, I looked at the art for sale. There was a poster with the words, *"Keep Calm and Stay Strong"* in bold letters. That seemed like good advice for me. *Was it a sign to calm down?* I wondered as I left the store. I stopped in a bookstore and, as I was passing the checkout counter, saw some magnets on display. One caught my eye. It said, *"Keep Calm and Stay Strong."* Again I read the same message, as if God was telling me not to worry.

Then I remembered a story from one of the issues of *Guideposts* magazine I had read recently. In it, a woman who was depressed got a "message" in the form of her favorite Bible verse in the same day, not once, but twice. Then she has the nerve to ask God for a third sign and got the same verse again!

I took the chance and followed suit. I asked God to show me the same message again. Later, I opened my purse and found a small bottle of essential oils I had forgotten was there. The bottle contained a blend of coriander, grapefruit, black pepper and ginger. I had used it in the past to share with my mother when she was in the hospital. When she was in pain, smelling the scent helped distract her. I had forgotten I had put that bottle in my purse to bring with me on the trip.

Guess what the label said? *"Calm Strength."* That was my third sign. I began to trust God would be in control. My brother called me the next day and offered to book our flight together. We were each other's moral support as we flew to be by our father's side.

You never know when God will show you a sign and all you have to do is ask! "Keep Calm and Stay Strong!"

Signs of Comfort

~ *Jill*

MY HUSBAND AND I got a call that his mother, who lived in a nursing home, had been in an accident. Because of the accident, her ribs and vertebrae were broken. The doctors told us that she would probably die within a day or two because the injuries made it difficult for her to breath.

At that time, my mother-in-law was in Kansas City, which is a nine-hour drive from where we lived. My husband and I quickly made arrangements for us to get off work and to make a trip to Kansas City. As we got ready, my husband packed a booklet that he and my mother-in-law had filled out years ago that stated her "end-of-life" wishes.

We drove through the night hoping to be there when she was still conscious and to support my sister-in-law who lived nearby. We arrived safely and in time. Although my mother-in-law could not say much, she recognized my husband (her son) and was glad to see him. Needless to say, it was difficult for us to see her suffer, but we were glad to be there with her. About 16 hours after we arrived, she passed away with my husband and his sister in the room with her. This was on a Friday evening.

The next day, a Saturday, we worked on funeral arrangements. In the booklet my mother-in-law had filled out, she had requested two specific things:

1. She wanted to be buried in Dubuque, Iowa in the cemetery next to her parents; and

2. The closing song for her funeral would be "How Great Thou Art."

How those two things worked out were amazing signs of comfort for us.

At first we were a little concerned about calling a church for a funeral in Dubuque. We had no family members living in that town and we had no associations with any of the parishes there. It was more than 65 years since my mother-in-law had lived in Dubuque! However, our daughter and her husband had gone to college in Dubuque and became friends with a classmate who later became a priest.

Our daughter called her friend, Fr. Alan, to ask him if he would preside for the funeral. Not only was he available for us, but we found out that his first assignment had been at the church where my mother-in-law had grown up! We were able to have the funeral at my mother-in-law's childhood parish which was comforting for all of us.

The Sunday between the death and the funeral, my husband and I went to Mass at the Catholic church near where we were staying in Kansas. Most of the songs for Mass were contemporary songs. However, the closing song was the very traditional song "How Great Thou Art," the song my mother-in-law had requested in her funeral arrangements! If that sign of comfort wasn't enough for us, instead of singing the first two verses, which usually is the case, we were asked to sing the first and last verses. The last verse is all about going home to God!

> *When Christ shall come, with shout of acclamation,*
> *And take me home, what joy shall fill my heart.*
> *Then I shall bow, in humble adoration,*
> *And then proclaim: "My God, how great Thou art!"*

A Journey in Patience

~ Lisa Diven

Wait on the Lord, be of good courage, and He will strengthen your heart. ~ Psalm 27:14

Patience is the fruit of the Spirit by which we live our daily lives in solid hope, love and trust, confident that God will cause His will to be done in us, for us and through us — in His good time and way.

MY HUSBAND AND I adopted Mayday, an adorable Jack Russell Terrier, five years ago. He had made his way to the shelter as a stray. He had sweaty paws and a bum knee but passed the meet-and-greet with our current dog and we excitedly took him home.

Our journey of emotions began when we discovered that Mayday suffered with severe separation anxiety.

He marked in our home, exhibited fear aggression, disliked people and cowered when you removed your shoes. He also was afflicted with severe allergies and didn't want to be held or accept affection.

It was clear that Mayday had not been socialized as a puppy and, unfortunately, his actions indicated that he also was abused. His faults were not *his* fault, and we couldn't help but wonder if someone gave up on and abandoned this little broken soul.

We attempted to cure Mayday holistically. We tried relaxation music, pheromone collars and infusers, anxiety jackets, male incontinence wraps and flower essences. We even hired a dog behaviorist to assess him.

"I suppose," my husband Todd remarked, "that anyone else would have just returned him to the shelter. I think he was brought into our lives for a reason."

My husband was right. We understood that most people would not have gone through such extremes but we had animal lover's hearts and the means to do so.

Over the years, Mayday had made small strides by growing to trust us and accepting our love but his behavior continued to go in waves until, for reasons unknown, he started marking on everything again.

Just like Mayday's behavior went in waves, so did our emotions. At first, we were disappointed and upset. Once we accepted him for what he was, and went through measures to help him to no avail, we experienced hope and frustration. When he started marking repeatedly, a great sadness grew inside us. And I must admit, as I tearfully shampooed urine out of carpet, too many times to count, I felt like a broken person as well.

"I can't take it anymore. I feel like I'm about to snap," I confessed to my husband. "I don't know what else we can do for him."

The dog had tried my patience and tested my tolerance and commitment. Would we ever be able to help Mayday? Perhaps we had failed him and ourselves. That's when we decided to discuss anxiety medications with our veterinarian. If medication would allow him to live a normal life, and in turn us as well, it was worth a try.

Years ago, in a church missalette, we received a postcard with the above Psalm and accompanying message of reflection. It reminded us of our pilgrimage with Mayday so we posted it on our refrigerator. It was often read when we needed encouragement and inspiration when caring for him.

In church on a recent Sunday, the pastor told the story of the little boy who wanted to buy a lame puppy. When the pet store owner offered to give the dog to him for free, he refused saying he'd pay for the dog in full because the dog that could not run and play was worth every bit as much as the dog that could. Then the boy revealed that he was crippled, too. The lame dog needed someone to love and care for him just as the little boy did.

Tears came to my eyes as the pastor relayed this message to the congregation. I couldn't help but think of Mayday. He was worthy of our unconditional love just as he has grown to provide us with his.

As we begin this "medicated journey" with our four-legged buddy, we accept that he will never be the perfect dog; just as we are not perfect. Even with his faults, Mayday has brought us joy and has taught us valuable lessons. And so we've discovered that sometimes it takes patience in life and in the Lord to heal a broken soul.

8

Answered Prayers

But they that wait upon the Lord
shall renew their strength; they shall mount up
with wings as eagles; they shall run, and not be weary;
and they shall walk, and not faint.

~ Isaiah 40:31

†

Help When You Need It Most

~ Mary Menzer

I THINK IT'S IMPORTANT for people to read this because God is so good and many of us just think these things happen by coincidence.

Basically my story is I worked part time while my kids were growing up. Actually my husband and I worked opposite shifts so we didn't have to pay for child care. It was a struggle, but things worked. Money was always tight, and luckily I had family who was able to help.

But you don't always want to keep asking for help.

I would pray about it and ask God for help, but usually the help came in such small ways that I never really thought about where that help was coming from. I chalked it up to just coincidence. But then one day, we had a large bill coming due, and the day before I had to pay it, there in my mail box was an unexpected check for almost exactly the amount we needed to pay.

This really got me to thinking that there was more to it than coincidence. I knew deep in my heart that God was answering my prayers and giving me just what I needed. As I look back this is what He's always done in my life, I just never realized it. He is so good!

Well, a few years ago, my middle daughter was in college and ready to do her student teaching—in Ireland!

Just before she left, I ran into an acquaintance who asked about the family and I told her about my daughter going to Ireland and she asked when I'm going to visit her. I explained that we just didn't have a trip to Ireland in the budget and I didn't even have a passport; she said she'd pray that God would find a way to make it happen.

She was one of those people who always said she'll pray for you and I'm pretty sure she means it.

I thanked her, because we can all use prayers, but really didn't think much of it.

Then I took my daughter to the airport—it was her first airplane ride and she was terrified. Not only was she terrified of the plane ride but also questioning why she thought she could fly halfway across the world by herself for the next six months. As I left her at the airport I felt like a terrible mom. What if she got sick or injured and she was there all alone and I couldn't go because I didn't have a passport?

Well, I decided then and there that I would at least apply for one. And, of course I tracked the flight on my computer and spent the night praying for her safety and praying that God would calm her fears. First thing in the morning, I went to the Post Office and applied for that passport.

A few minutes after I got home, my phone rings and it's another friend from the neighborhood looking to see if one of my girls could babysit. When I mentioned that Nicole was in Ireland, she said she had forgotten and she asked when (not if) we were going to see her. Again, I had to say that we just could not afford such a trip. She then said, "Why didn't you ask me?"

"Well I don't usually ask friends to send us on European vacations!" I answered. To which she replied, "Well, my husband's a pilot and can get you a buddy pass."

I thought buddy passes were only for immediate family, but I guess I was wrong.

Anyway, to make a long story short, I was able to use one of those buddy passes. My husband was not able to take off work, so my sister went with, also on a buddy pass! My sister and I were both able to fly round trip (and even first class!) to spend a wonderful week that I will never forget with my daughter.

I know God heard all those prayers and put the right people in my life at just the right times to make it happen. When I look back, I believe He has been doing this all my life and I believe He does it for all of us. We just need to "let go and let God." I shared this story because I hope others will choose to trust Him and see what He'll do for them.

The Faith of a Mustard Seed

~ Susan Schuerr

IT WAS CHRISTMAS TIME and we were excited about flying to beautiful Bozeman, Montana, to see our daughter Deborah and our son Aaron and his family. We had a pleasant place to reside while we visited for ten days.

Our daughter arranged for us to stay at her friend John's house. He was visiting his family in Washington so the house was available. It didn't take long for us to settle in. We could drive the car into the attached garage and walk up a couple steps into the cozy dining room.

We quickly changed into our cross-country clothes and waxed our skis for a day at Hyalite National Forest. Skiing in Hyalite is like being in a holiday postcard. The snow is deep and well-packed, the trails take us through snow-covered pine trees, and the clouds cut through the surrounding mountains while the sun peeks through, making the snow glow gold like specks from Rumpelstiltskin spinning wheel.

It was a very special day. We were meeting Aaron, his wife Lynelle and our 18-month-old grandson, August. I was entering our car in the garage while Larry, whose 6-foot-2-inch frame filled the doorway, said, "Looks like we have everything." He then shut the door only to realize that he had left the key to the house on the dining room table.

"What should we do now?" I said.

I could envision our flight tickets and key on the table so far from our grasp. We walked around the house checking ways to enter, possibly through a window unlocked, etc. We looked for a hidden key but the place was like Fort Knox, no viewed entrance. So we had a choice to either spend the day figuring out how to deal with our dilemma or going on and enjoying the day. I said a prayer that went like this: "God, you see our problem and in faith I turn to you for a solution. I trust that you will give us wisdom to deal with this situation." We then kept our date with our son and his young family.

My joy returned to me at the sight of little August who could speak in whole sentences. August grinned with delight flying up and down the hills on the sled my son pulled behind him. After an hour or so, he looked up at us with his green mischievous eyes and orange hair sticking out of his cap saying, "Walk a bit, walk a bit." He escaped his cocoon of enclosed blankets and began examining the new substance called "snow." We threw a few snowballs while munching on delicious homemade revel bars.

As shades of pink streaked the sky, we headed back to our cars. I kissed my dear first grandson's frozen chubby red cheeks and headed to the car. It was a perfect winter day filled with joy and delight. But now as we drove circumspectly into the attached garage, our dilemma returned. *How were we going to get into our house without a key?*

After inspecting the house once again, Larry said, "I might have to dismantle the door." Being an industrial arts teacher and former contractor I knew he could probably do it with tools—but we had none. I also worried about damaging the house so graciously offered to us. Once again, I prayed for God to help us and give us wisdom. It says in the Bible, "My sheep hear my voice and follow me."

In a whisper, an impression came to me: "Try your home key."

It sounded absurd but why not, I thought. What have we got to lose?

Larry reluctantly took our house key from my hand and tried fitting it in the lock. We held our breath as he slowly turned the key and voila—it opened the door. We were astounded. Like two little kids on a new trampoline, we jumped and shouted with glee.

Who would have guessed that our home key in Illinois would fit in the doorknob of a house in Bozeman, Montana? It was proof that our heavenly Father heard our prayers and that He saw our faith in Him to deliver us from ourselves. He certainly is Abba Father—one who takes care of his children.

The Ring

~ Nina F.

DURING THE VIETNAM WAR, my father was getting ready to be shipped out. He had been dating my mother and wanted to marry her. She wanted to wait until he got back so he gave her a promise ring. It was a silver band, oval on top with small diamond chips.

She wore that ring and after he got back, they were married. She still wore the ring throughout their marriage until I got married and then she gave it to me, her daughter. I was afraid I would lose it if I wore it every day and only wore it on special occasions like holidays.

On Father's Day 2005, I called my aunt and asked what she needed for the party at her house. She asked me to bring an appetizer so I went to the store and bought some food. When I got to her house, we had our celebration; all the while I wasn't aware I had lost the ring.

That night, I forgot about the ring but then later realized I didn't have it. I called my aunt to ask if she saw it at her house. She looked for a few days and it was nowhere to be found. A friend suggested I rent a metal detector which I did.

I started praying day and night until I found the ring. I prayed to St. Anthony, "Tony, Tony, turn around, something's lost and must be found ....help me to find my mother's silver ring."

By now, a week had gone by and I was worried it was never going to be found. Just as I pulled up to the front of my aunt's house, with my metal detector in the car, I noticed in the middle of the street a shiny object. My ring!

It must have fallen off the day I came to her party and lay there for week! What are the odds that it stayed there and no one saw it or that it hadn't been moved by some car going by?

My uncle said, "You are blessed." I believe it.

Canoe Trip

~ Gary Renard

I STARED AT THE map on my wall studying the two-mile stretch of the creek which I'd left unexplored with my canoe. Only two more miles and my task would be complete!

The week before, canoeing the previous section of this creek had been an absolute disaster. The creek had wound through a wild area of bush, fallen trees and several beaver dams. I had to push, pull and drag the canoe over one obstacle after another. At the end of my experience, I was exhausted, wet, caked with mud and bitten up by deer flies.

How could I be considering putting myself through the same ordeal again?

According to my U.S.G.S. map, everything west of Jackson road was a wild area. The creek broke into a series of squiggles and even divided into two streams, winding through marshy islands. If I liked last weeks' torturous experience, then I would just love this, I thought, but I knew I had to do it.

The day before my trip, I offered a prayer: "Lord, here I am ready to push myself into this crazy ordeal. Well, how about this?

All the struggle, discomfort and mess that I will be going through, let me offer it all to You. It's a pretty lame gift, but I hope You can find some way to use it. At least this will teach me not to be so foolishly stubborn in the future."

The next day, I pushed my canoe into the final stretch of the creek, and as I paddled apprehensively under the Jackson Road bridge, I thought, "OK, here it comes." Then, nothing! During the next mile and a half, the creek ran straight and deep. Several years after my map had been printed, the channel had been dredged and straightened. I paddled eagerly through in half an hour.

When I was finished, I loaded my canoe onto my car, and looked back at the creek. I remembered my prayer. "I wasn't able to offer You anything," I thought.

In a moment, I understood. This was His way of offering to me.

Contributors

About Joyce Kocinski

Ever since her father told her the story of how his guardian angel carried him through the snow-covered minefield to answer the call "Medic! Medic!" Joyce Kocinski has believed in angels.

As a soldier in World War II, Kocinski's father saw action in Europe. In France, he earned the Silver Star and Bronze Star for rescuing wounded soldiers while his company was under attack. In Colmar, France, he found the dog tags of a French soldier with the last 4 digits 1137 (the same last numbers of his dog tags). He eventually earned the Purple Heart award for being wounded in battle when he was shot in the leg by a German sniper (outside of Colmar!).

Stories like the one told by Kocinski's father led her to the creation of this book. We all have stories in our lives that show Divine intervention.

Joyce Kocinski is a retired special education teacher and has a Master's degree in education. She is an adjunct teacher at the local community college. She also teaches workshops in writing and journaling to organizations. Her blog, *One Day at a Time,* shares insights on topics about faith and family. Her first book, *Letters from Mom: A Daughter's Journal of Healing,* is based on a journal she

MORE THAN A COINCIDENCE

started the year after her mother died to help process her grief. To follow news about her books and blog posts, check out http://joycekocinski.wordpress.com.

Perhaps you have a story of Divine intervention to share. Contact Joyce Kocinski at jkocinski@wowway.com for more information.

About Jennifer Burgsteiner

Jennifer Burgsteiner, a resident of Algonquin, Illinois, is a wife, blessed mother of three, CPA and Stampin' Up Demonstrator.

About Lisa Diven

Lisa Diven lives in West Dundee, Illinois, with her Harley-riding husband Todd and four rescued pets. Her true passion is writing fiction but she moonlights as a marketing writer. She dabbles in freelance writing and is an avid supporter of Anderson Animal Shelter, through which many of her articles have been featured. Extending her love for the written word, she's a member of the Fox Valley Writers Group and leads the Writers on the Fox; a creative writing group at the Gail Borden Public Library, Elgin, Illinois. Buy the Fox Valley Writers Group Anthologies via Amazon/ Kindle: *Foxtales I, Foxtales II* or *Foxtales III.*

About Cinnamon Kettner

Cinnamon Kettner is from Huntley, Illinois. She is a loving mother of three. Cinnamon and her husband Joe started a Foundation, *cancer kiss my cooley,* in honor of their son Carter, forever 6 and too beautiful for earth. She shares her love of God openly with anybody who will listen and enjoys her part-time businesses,

Tastefully Simple and Mary Kay, with everybody who she feels she can help improve their lives, in any way that she can. Contact Cinnamon at ckettner@cancerkissmycooley.org or sageinbloom @att.net.

About Debra Kollar

Debra Kollar grew up in South Bend, Indiana, and is a Purdue graduate in Public Relations and Speech Education. She lives in Illinois with her husband, two children, five cats, and a 14-year-old dog. She worked as a columnist for Catholic Charities and has been published in the anthology, *Naturally Yours.* To read more of her life stories go to www.soyouwouldthink.blogspot.com.

About Deede Krage

Deede Krage lives in Northern Illinois with her best friend and husband of thirty-two years. She has three children and two grand-children. She is a member of the Algonquin Area Writers Group. This is her first published short story.

About Rosemary Larson

Rosemary Larson is a mother of five, graduated college when her youngest began kindergarten and then became a professional fundraiser for non-profits for 30 years retiring five years ago.

About Monica Lee

Monica Lee, author of *The Percussionist's Wife: A Memoir of Sex, Crime & Betrayal,* is an editor, blogger and freelance writer whose work has appeared in the newspapers, marketing materials and blogs during the past two and half decades. She also designed the cover, e-book and paperback interior for *More Than a Coincidence: True Stories of Divine Intervention.*

Read reviews of memoirs and more about her own memoir, writing and self-publishing at her writing blog (www.mindfulmonica.wordpress.com) or follow her everyday life at her Minnesota Transplant blog (www.minnesotatransplant.wordpress.com). She lives in northern Illinois with her second husband.

About Patrick J. Murphy III

Patrick J. Murphy III recently returned to the Chicago area. He attended the Ohio State University for Theater and is working towards being a director. Writing for Patrick had always been a hobby, and he is happy to see a work published. Currently he is working on a young adult novel featuring witches, wizards, and warlocks.

About Julie Ostrow

As a Humor, Laughter, and Improv Coach, American Laughing Champion and Second City-trained Julie Ostrow teaches organizations and corporate teams to use Improv 2 Improve to improve creativity, communication, team building, and innovation with their clients and within their organizations. As a certified laughter yoga leader, she conducts humor and laughter workshops in which she teaches the benefits of using humor and laughter in all aspects of our lives, including in the workplace.

Julie's tips for incorporating humor, laugher, and improvisation into our lives is featured in the upcoming book, *The Best of Happiness Recipe Radio, Year One.*

Copies of this book will be available at www.GoFindTheFunny.com.

Book Julie for your next team building meeting or event! Contact her at Julie@GoFindTheFunny.com or (847) 946-4343.

About Peg Ricketts

Peg Ricketts is from Omaha, Nebraska. She is married with four adult children and two granddaughters. She is an active volunteer at St. Philip Neri Church, American Cancer Society's "Look Good Feel Better" program for female cancer patients and the Leukemia Lymphoma Society.

About Leticia Rivera Davis

Leticia Rivera Davis is a U.S. Army Retired Master Sergeant, experienced Spanish teacher and aspiring writer. Her poor upbringing in Brooklyn, New York, and her valued family ties to Puerto Rico are themes for her journeys in the military, teaching and memoir writing. She holds a BA in Distributed Studies (English, Spanish, and Communications) and an MA in Curriculum and Instruction. She currently lives in Georgia and substitute teaches near her home. She wrote a story entitled "The Treasure of Books," previously published in *Back To School: 2013 Memoir Anthology* edited by Karen Hamilton Silvestri. She also travels frequently to visit family and friends in New York, Kentucky and Puerto Rico. If you'd like to connect with her, send email to letrausa.rivera@gmail.com.

About Suzi Sandoval

Suzi Sandoval is a writer and an award-winning speaker. She is spokesperson for MADD and Victims Impact Panel for the Potter County Prosecutor's Office in Amarillo, Texas. She also speaks for

Life Gift, educating audiences on the importance of organ donation. She is a founding member of The Lone Star Haiku Poets Society and immediate-past president of Toastmasters. She has been recognized as a class communicator by CLASSEMINARS, Inc. Suzi is in the process of writing her memoir and hopes to publish it by November 2015. For more information about her memoir contact Suzi at suzisandoval9@gmail.com.

About Susan Schuerr

Susan Schuerr has been published in three anthologies: *Ignite Your Passion: Seek Your Peak to Find Your Spark* by April M. Williams, *Falling in Love with You* by Oak Tara Publishers and now Joyce Kocinski's *More Than a Coincidence: True Stories of Divine Intervention.* She also was featured in the Love Notes section of the Chicago Tribune. She is an educator, writer and speaker. In her spare time she loves to bike, ski, and play the piano. Sue lives in Fox River Grove, Illinois, with her husband Larry. They have three adult children and five grandchildren. She writes regularly at her blog entitled www.lifewithlarry.org where she shares often humorously about their marriage, adventures and service projects.

If you enjoyed this book, please consider leaving a review at Amazon or wherever your buy your books, even it's only a line or two. It helps get the word out about this book and the authors who contributed, and it would be very much appreciated.

Made in the USA
Lexington, KY
10 March 2018